Presented to

Missy Mac

by

Gamma K.

on

May 26, 2006.

09 08 07 06 05   9 8 7 6 5 4 3

MY LITTLE GOOD NIGHT PRAYERS

written by Susan L. Lingo

illustrated by Kathy Parks

Standard Publishing

cincinnati, ohio

Contents

New Testament

Prayer Time Rhyme

Come, let's share a prayer,

a prayer, a prayer—

Come, let's share a prayer

and talk to our Lord.

To say, "God, I love you,"

And tell God "I thank you;"

Oh, come, let's share a prayer

and talk to our Lord.

Hi, I'm Night-Light,
your special firefly friend!

Come with me as I help you to remember
some of my favorite Bible stories. Then
we will spend quiet time
together with God. We'll
pray to him and praise
him, too—thanking him for
all the neat things he
does! My ladybug pal
will always be
somewhere in every
Bible story picture. Be
sure to look for her!
Let's get started!

Who made the world such a special place to be?
What do you enjoy about God's creation?

God Made the World

God said, "I made the earth." Isaiah 45:12

A Story to Read

Who made the world? God made the world. God made the world a nice place to be and added such beauty for you and for me! Only God is wise enough and powerful enough to make a whole world. Only God is our Creator. And what a wonderful world God made for us: flowers, birds, and bees that buzz; oceans and stars and dandelion fuzz.

When God made the world, he added many special touches. God added colors like red, blue, green, and yellow. Can you find all the yellow flowers and the orange caterpillar? Only God can make a world! How do we know? The Bible tells us so!

Isaiah 45:12

A Song to Sing

God made the world in seven days. Can you count to seven? 1, 2, 3, 4, 5, 6, 7! Let's sing a special song about all the gifts God gave us on every day he created.

CREATION SONG

(tune: *Old McDonald*)

On the first day God made light—
Thank you, thank you, Lord!
God made light and it was good—
Thank you, thank you, Lord!

With light, light here, and light, light there—
Here is light, there is light, everywhere is light, light!
On the first day God made light—
Thank you, thank you, Lord!

On the second day God made air . . .
On the third day God made land . . .
On the fourth day God made stars . . .
On the fifth day God made animals . . .
On the sixth day God made people . . .
On the seventh day God took a rest . . .

What things in Night-Light's basket did God create?

A Prayer to Pray

Let's praise God for making the world so good and beautiful. After each line say, "God is good."

God made the flowers and the buzzy bees,
> *God is good.*

God made the birds to nest in the trees.
> *God is good.*

God made the mighty mountains tall,
> *God is good.*

And fuzzy-wuzzy caterpillars sweet and small.
> *God is good.*

God made the winds and the rains fly free.
> *God is good.*

God made the world for you and ME!
> *God is good.*

Here's a prayer for you to pray to thank our Creator for his loving way!

Dear God, we know you made the earth
And all the stars above—
You made the world then added us
So you'd have someone to love! Amen.

Point to and name all the colors in the rainbow.
Why did God put a rainbow in the sky for Noah?

Perfect Promises

God said, "What God promises, he keeps." Numbers 23:19

A Story to Read

Here's a fun riddle for you. What does God give away yet always keep? His promises! God gives his promises to us and always keeps them, too. God promised Noah it would rain—and it rained. God promised Noah the rain would stop—and it stopped. And God promised Noah he'd be safe—and Noah was kept safe. Then God put a rainbow in the sky as a sign of his promise never to flood the world again. What a pretty way to remember God's promises!

Why does God make promises? Because he loves us! And because God loves us, he keeps every promise he makes. How do we know? The Bible tells us so!

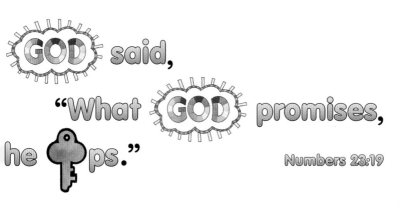

A Game to Play

I love birthdays, don't you? People give us gifts on our birthdays because they love us. It's the same with God's gifts, too. God helps us and gives us special gifts because he loves us! Just as God gave Noah the special gifts of his love and promises, God gives us those wonderful gifts, too.

Let's give God a big "thank you," to show him our love, too!

Show God your love and thank him for the things on the flower petals. Now think: what else can you thank God for?

A Prayer to Pray

Point to each color in the rainbow. Then after each praise, say, "Thank you, God."

Red is for apples you made taste just right,
Thank you, God.
Orange is for sunsets all fiery and bright.
Thank you, God.
Yellow's for buttercups, tiny but great,
Thank you, God.
Green is for peas that roll on my plate!
Thank you, God.
Blue is the sky, like an ocean of air,
Thank you, God.
Purple are flowers that bloom everywhere!
Thank you, God.
For the rainbow of things you promise to do,
We praise you, and say, "Thank you!"

Here's a prayer for you to pray to thank God for his promises every day.

Dear God, your love is so very deep,
The promises you make, you keep.
We're thankful we can trust in you
And in your perfect promises, too! Amen.

Why did God tumble the tower of Babel?
How many red bricks do you see?

The One and Only

God said, "Remember that I am God." Isaiah 46:9

A Story to Read

Do you remember the Tower of Babel and the people who built it so high? The people thought they could be as wise as God if their tower touched the sky. But only God is wisest of all, so he tumbled that tower—oh my!

The people who built the Tower of Babel thought they were smart. But they were oh, so wrong! If they had learned God's Word, they would have learned that only God is wiser than anyone. They would have learned that only God is more powerful than anyone. And they would have learned that we are to honor and praise only God! How do we know? The Bible tells us so!

GOD said, "Remember that am GOD."

Isaiah 46:9

A Game to Play

When we want to learn about God, he helps us. God helps us learn his Word. God helps us learn ways to praise him. And God helps us pray, too.

Pretend to unwrap your special gift from God. Now put on your thinking cap and let's see what you've learned!

 Who is wiser than anyone? *God!*

 Who controls the stars and sun? *God!*

 Who hears our prayers each day and night? *God!*

 Who do we love with all our might? *God!*

A Prayer to Pray

Let's praise God for being so wise by using our hands in a fun way.

Not just small praise—
(hands at shoulders)
Give God TALL praise!
(hands high in the air)
Praise that reaches way up high—
(point upward)
Praise so tall it taps the sky!
(jump and point upward)
We praise God because he's wise—
(tap your head)
Lift your hands, let your praises rise!
(stretch hands in the air)

Let's honor God with a prayer to thank him for being smarter and stronger than anyone.

Dear God, you are the only one
Who rules the night and commands the sun.
Please let us know, please open our eyes,
To see that only you are strong or wise! Amen.

Point to the items Abraham may have taken on his trip.
What items would you take on a trip?

Just Trust!

God said, "They will trust in the Lord." Zephaniah 3:12

A Story to Read

Moving to a new home can be fun, but it can be a little scary, too. Will I like my new home or the friends I meet there? Will I still have my bed and my favorite chair?

That's what Abraham felt when God told him to move to a new home. Abraham wasn't sure about moving, so he prayed and asked God's help. Then Abraham trusted God and followed him. Abraham knew God would take care of him in his new home. And God did! Abraham trusted and believed in God's care, and liked his new home when he finally got there! We can trust God, too. How do we know? The Bible tells us so!

GOD said, "They will trust the Lord."

Zephaniah 3:12

A Song to Sing

Can you find the gift with the word "trust" on it? Trusting God is like a special gift from God to us. Let's sing a song about trusting God. You can point to the letters in the word "trust" as we sing.

TRUST

(tune: *Bingo*)

We always know
what God will do

Because he tells us
and it's true—

T-R-U-S-T
T-R-U-S-T
T-R-U-S-T

Have trust, you really must!

What gift did God give Abraham
that he also gives you?

A Prayer to Pray

Trusting God means we know he will do what he promises. We really must trust God every day and night, and God will help us through his power and might! Let's praise God for the trust he helps us have. After each line shout, "Trust, trust, we really must!"

For God's help in all we do,
Trust, trust, we really must!
For God's love toward me and you,
Trust, trust, we really must!
For every time God hears a prayer,
Trust, trust, we really must!
We praise you, God, for being there!
Trust, trust, we really must!

Let's offer God a thank-you prayer for helping us to trust him and for being there!

Dear God, it feels so good to trust in you
'Cuz we know you'll help us in all we do.
Please help us have trust in a really big way,
So we can follow you every day! Amen.

Who protected baby Moses? How many flowers and butterflies do you see by the river?

Safe and Sound

God said, "I will save you." Jeremiah 30:10

A Story to Read

Cuddle in your blankets, now cuddle down. Don't you feel all safe and sound? Being held or cuddled is nice, isn't it? It makes us feel warm and loved and very safe.

That's how baby Moses felt when his mommy put him in a snug basket. Moses' mommy knew that God would keep her baby safe and sound, cuddled and warm; that God would protect her baby and keep him from harm. God protected baby Moses and God promises to watch over us and keep us safe, too. How do we know? The Bible tells us so!

GOD said, " will save U."

Jeremiah 30:10

A Rhyme to Say

Why does God give us the gift of being safe each day and night? It's because God loves us very much and holds us close and tight! God's gift of being safe and sound shows that God loves us.

Now let's say a rhyme about how God keeps us safe.

**Safe and sound,
safe and sound—**

**God is watching
all around.**

**God keeps us safe
both night and day—**

**So we're safe and sound
in every way!**

What happened to Moses after God kept him safe? God will keep you safe because he loves you, too!

A Prayer to Pray

How do you keep your milk safe and sound with no spills? You watch over your cup! You watch over your cup and try not to tip it as you enjoy your milk and happily sip it. God keeps us safe by watching over us, too.

Let's praise and thank God for keeping us safe with a fun rhyme. Put on your pretend binoculars and look at all the things God sees.

**God watches over the good night moon,
God watches over my little room.
God watches over my cozy bed
And the puffy pillow where I lay my head.
God watches over my favorite toys
And knows what makes each nighttime noise.
God watches over me all through the night,
So I am safe and sleep so tight.**

Let's ask God to watch over us throughout the day and night.

**Dear God, we pray and ask of you
To keep us safe in all we do.
Stay above us,
Always love us. Amen.**

Find Moses' staff. How did God use Moses' staff to keep his people safe? Count the fish in the sea.

Safe in God's Love

God said, "I will save you." Jeremiah 30:10

A Story to Read

From a burning bush God asked Moses to keep his people safe from a king who was oh, so mean. And what do you think Moses said when God asked him to help? Moses said, "I'll be God's helper—special and true—and do all the things God tells me to do!

So Moses freed God's people and ran from the king who was oh, so mean, until they came to the big, deep sea. How could Moses get across as safe as safe can be? God helped Moses! God parted that sea and kept Moses safe as safe could be. God keeps us safe and sound, too! How do we know? The Bible tells us so!

GOD said, "I will save U."

Jeremiah 30:10

A Song to Sing

I can trust God to guard me and guide me and stay right beside me. Let's sing a fun song to thank God for loving us and saving us.

SAFE AND SOUND
(tune: *Row Your Boat*)

Run, run, Moses run
(run in place)
As fast as you can flee—
God will keep you safe and sound
Just as he does for me!

Walk, walk, Moses walk
(walk in place)
Across the parted sea—
God will keep you safe and sound
Just as he does for me!

Smile, smile, Moses smile
(smile and point upward)
Safe as safe can be—
God has kept you safe from harm
Just as he does for me!

Find the shadows.
Name the shapes.

A Prayer to Pray

Let's praise God for keeping us safe by saying, "God saves us!" at the end of each line.

Who saves us through his power?
God saves us!
Who saves us through his might?
God saves us!
Who keeps us safe within his love day and night?
God saves us!
Who can we trust to help us?
God saves us!
Who will always guide us?
God saves us!
Who keeps us safe and always stays beside us?
God saves us!

Now we thank God with a prayer for keeping us safe and sound.

Dear God, we pray and ask of you
To hold us safe in all we do.
Stay above us,
Always love us. Amen.

How many stone tablets did God use for his rules?

Rules Rule!

God said, "Obey me." Jeremiah 7:23

A Story to Read

There are rules at home and rules at school. There are rules at church and at the playground. Why are there rules we have to obey? To keep us happy and safe at work or play! God gave us the most important rules to obey. God gave us ten important rules called the Ten Commandments. Can you count to ten? 1-2-3-4-5-6-7-8-9-10. Ten rules God gave us to always obey; ten rules to follow in every way.

We can obey God by praying and thanking him and learning his Word. God wants us to choose to obey him! How do we know? The Bible tells us so!

GOD said,

"Obey me."

Jeremiah 7:23

A Song to Sing

Whenever we do what we're told to do, we obey. When we obey God in all that we do, what a nice way to say, "I love you!"

Let's sing a fun song to God about obeying. You can march and clap in time to the tune.

ALWAYS OBEY
(tune: *Three Blind Mice*)

Always obey! Always obey!
In all you do! And all you say!

Whenever we mind the way God wants us to,
And mind our Mommies and Daddies, too;

We'll bring smiles of love in all we do—
Always obey! Always obey!

Find Night-Light's signs: Stop, Go, Don't Walk, One Way. What does each sign mean?

A Prayer to Pray

Let's learn about the Ten Commandments as we praise God with this fun rhyme. Hold up the right number of fingers every time you hear a number word.

Ten rules God gave us to always obey;
Ten rules to follow in every way.
Rule 1—God is our only God.
Rule 2—Worship God, the only one.
Rule 3—Always love and respect God's name.
Rule 4—Take a rest from all your fun.
Rule 5—Love your mommy and daddy.
Rule 6—Never hurt anyone.
Rule 7—Husbands and wives be true to each
other.
Rule 8—Never steal from anyone.
Rule 9—Please don't ever tell a lie.
Rule 10—Be happy with what you own.

Let's thank God for his ten special rules with a special prayer.

Dear God, thank you for the ten special rules
You gave us to always obey—
Please help us follow each important rule
As well as we can each day. Amen.

How did God help Joshua?
Count the orange stones in the wall.

A Tower of Help and Power

God said, "I will help you." Isaiah 41:10

A Story to Read

Try to lift the corner of your bed. Ugh! It's too heavy for only one; you need help to get the job done! Ask Mommy or Daddy to help you and you will see that a helping hand is what you need.

Joshua had a big job to do. Joshua and God's soldiers needed to get over the walls of Jericho. But me-oh-my, those walls were tall—how could the soldiers get over them all? Joshua asked God to help him. Then Joshua followed God's directions. Joshua and God's soldiers marched around, and with God's help, the walls fell down—ta-daa! We can count on God when we ask him for help. How do we know? The Bible tells us so!

GOD said, "I will help U."

Isaiah 41:10

41

A Rhyme to Say

When we need help throughout our days, God gives us help in many ways. How does God help us? Let's find out!

God helps us grow up straight and tall,
(stand up tall)
And helps by answering when we call.
(shout, "I love you, God!")
God helps us when we're feeling bad,
(look sad)
And turns our hearts from sad to glad.
(smile)
God helps us say our prayers at night,
(fold hands in prayer)
And helps us sleep so sweet and tight!
(pretend to sleep)

Point to the face that shows how you feel. No matter how you feel today, God will help you in every way.

A Prayer to Pray

Think of all the sevens in the story of Joshua and the giant walls of Jericho. There were seven priests with seven horns and God's soldiers marched for seven morns. Around they marched seven times in all and when the horns tooted, down came the walls! We can have fun counting to seven and remembering God's powerful help.

1-2-3-4-5-6-7—7 priests followed Joshua.
(march in place)
1-2-3-4-5-6-7—7 horns they blew, TA-DAA!
(blow pretend horns)
1-2-3-4-5-6-7—7 times they marched around;
(march in place)
Then through God's power the walls fell down!
TA-DAA!
(blow pretend horns)

Now here's a prayer for us to say to thank God for his powerful help each day.

Dear God, you're more powerful than anyone
And with your help we can get the job done.
We give you thanks for the help and love
You send our way from heaven above. Amen.

What is Night-Light sharing with his friends?
Who was Naomi's friend?

Fine Friends

God said, "Love your neighbor." Leviticus 19:18

A Story to Read

Who loves to stop and play awhile? Who always leaves you with a smile? Who is so friendly? Why, your friends, of course! Ruth and Naomi were best friends. They helped and shared with one another and showed God's love to each other. Naomi told Ruth all about God and Ruth shared her food with Naomi.

Think of all the friends you have: friends you meet at the swimming pool, friends in church, friends at school. Your family is full of friendly friends—just think of all the love God sends! God wants us to love our friends and neighbors and show them his love, too. How do we know? The Bible tells us so!

GOD said, "LOVE your neighbor."

Leviticus 19:18

A Song to Sing

Why were Ruth and Naomi such good friends? They were good friends because they loved God and they cared for each other. I like doing nice things for my friends and showing them my love. It makes me feel so cozy and happy inside.

Let's sing a happy song for God and our friends.

THE KINDNESS SONG

(tune: *Ten Little Indians*)

**Be kind and loving to one another,
Be forgiving of each other—**

**Show your love in all you do
'Cuz that's how God loves you!**

How many friends are with Night-Light?

A Prayer to Pray

Cut out two paper hearts. Hold your paper hearts and tell the names of two friends. Let's praise and thank God for friends to care for and friends to love, for all the friends God sends from above! Toss a paper heart in the air and say, "We thank you, Lord!" after each praise.

We praise you for friends who care for us;
We thank you, Lord.
We praise you for friends who share with us.
We thank you, Lord.
We praise you for every person you send;
We thank you, Lord.
We praise you for being our best friend!
We thank you, Lord.

Here's a prayer for us to say to thank God for sending friends our way.

Dear God, we're glad you send to us
Friends who love and care for us.
Please help us be kind to every friend
Whom you take the time to send. Amen.

How many stones did David have for his sling?
How many stones did David need to bring
down Goliath with God's help?

48

Giant Strength

God said, "I will make you strong." Isaiah 45:5

A Story to Read

Some things seem impossible to do. It seemed impossible for small David to fight giant Goliath. But even though David was small, his love for God was oh-so-tall! David asked God to make him strong, and what happened then? David swung his sling 'round and 'round, and—zing! plop!—Goliath fell down!

If you're afraid of thunder, who helps you be strong? And when you're feeling not-so-brave, who helps you get along? You may have lots of people who love and help you, but no one is as big or strong as God is! God will always help you be strong when you ask him. How do we know? The Bible tells us so!

A Game to Play

The ceiling is way up high, isn't it? Mean old Goliath was even taller than the ceiling! But was Goliath bigger than God? Oh, no! God is bigger and stronger than anyone or anything. Isn't it wonderful to know that our bigger-than-anything God helps us and makes us strong? Here are words for you to shout and let your joy for God's strength come out!

Let us shout!
Let us sing!
God is bigger than anything!
We can go to any length
With God's power and his strength!

Find David (he's the smallest brother). Find these brothers: the curly-haired, the tallest, and the oldest.

A Prayer to Pray

David wasn't very big; he was really sort of small—but when he asked for God to help, his strength grew really tall! David learned that God makes us strong and brave. Let's praise God for his help and strength with a fun action rhyme.

Can you clap your hands today?
I can do it right away!
(clap hands)
I can go to any length
When I ask God for help and strength!

(repeat using the following questions and actions.)
- **Can you stomp your feet today?**
- **Can you twirl around today?**
- **Can you touch your toes today?**

Here's a prayer that we can pray to ask God for strength every day.

Dear God, we ask you for strength
To live for you each day.
Please help us grow so strong and brave
In all we do and say. Amen.

Who heard and answered Daniel's prayers?
How many lions do you see?

Powerful Prayers

God said, "I will answer you." Jeremiah 33:3

A Story to Read

Who's never too busy or makes us fuss, and takes the time to answer us? God! God hears our prayers, each and all, and always answers when we call! Daniel called upon God when the mean king wanted Daniel to pray to him instead of God.

Naughty, naughty! Mean King Darius was going to toss Daniel into a cave of lions! But Daniel said, "Dear God, I'll only pray to you no matter what men say or do." Growly-scowly lions snarled at Daniel as he prayed and asked God for help. God heard and answered Daniel on that growly night and closed the lions' jaws up tight! God hears and answers us, too. How do we know? The Bible tells us so.

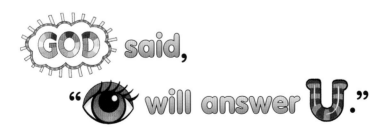

GOD said,

"👁 will answer U."

Jeremiah 33:3

A Song to Sing

God is never too busy to hear each little payer I pray, no matter if it's night or day! And God answers me in his time and way because he loves me! Just as God answered Daniel when he prayed, God answers our prayers, too.

Let's sing a happy song to thank God for taking the time to hear and answer us.

GOD WILL ANSWER
(tune: *Jesus Loves Me*)

God will hear and answer us
Because he loves and cares for us—
God will answer in his way
When we bow our hearts to pray.
Yes, God will answer—
Yes, God will answer—
Yes, God will answer—
Because he loves us so.

Who is praying with Night-Light?
How many buttons can you count?

A Prayer to Pray

Let's say this rhyme to praise God for answering us when we pray.

I don't care what people say,
(shake your head and finger)
I want to pray to God each day!
(make prayer hands)
I'll praise and honor God through prayer,
(make prayer hands)
No matter when—no matter where!
(shake your head and finger)
God will hear and answer me
(point upward)
'Cuz that's what God promises me!
(hand on your heart)

Here's a prayer for us to say to thank God for answering when we pray!

Dear God, you hear all that we say
When we bow our hearts to pray.
Thank you for answering in your way,
And for your loving help each day. Amen.

What happened to Jonah when he tried to hide from God? How many starfish do you see?

56

God Answers Us

God said, "I will answer you." Jeremiah 33:3

A Story to Read

Cover your head with your pillow—oops! I can't see you! But, who knows you're there and sees you all the time? God!

Jonah tried to hide from God, but did it work? No siree! God saw Jonah and heard every word he prayed—even when the giant fish swallowed him! God heard Jonah say, "I'm sorry." God heard Jonah say, "Help me." And God answered Jonah's prayers as quickly as could be! Pfftooey! The fish spit Jonah on the sand and Jonah learned a giant lesson in the way God sees, and hears, and answers us. God is always with us and hears each word we say. And because God loves us, he answers when we pray. How do we know? The Bible tells us so!

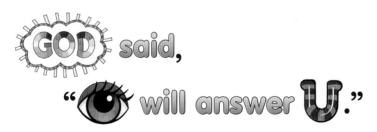

GOD said, "I will answer U."

Jeremiah 33:3

A Song to Sing

God shows his love for us by listening to all we say and by answering every prayer we pray. Fold your hands as if to pray and sing to God in a special way.

GOD WILL ANSWER
(tune: *Jesus Loves Me*)

**God will hear and answer us
Because he loves and cares for us—
God will answer in his way
When we bow our hearts to pray.
Yes, God will answer—
Yes, God will answer—
Yes, God will answer—
Because he loves us so.**

Find the biggest fish that swallowed Jonah. Point to the smallest fish, the striped fish, and the pink fish.

A Prayer to Pray

Let's praise and thank God for listening to us all and for answering us when we call.

I don't need a walkie-talkie;
    (pretend to talk on a walkie-talkie)
I don't need to dial a phone.
    (pretend to dial a telephone)
I don't need to type an e-mail;
    (pretend to type a keyboard)
I don't need a microphone.
    (pretend to hold a microphone)
When I want to talk with God, all I do is pray,
    (make prayer hands)
And God will answer me 24 hours a day!
    (jump and cheer)

Let's share a prayer that God will hear because he loves us and he's near.

Dear God, I'm glad you always answer us
Because you love and care for us.
I'm glad you lend your loving ear
And that you answer because you're near. Amen.

What did baby Jesus sleep in the night he was born? Name all the animals you can find.

Here and Near

God said, "I am with you." Jeremiah 30:11

A Story to Read

God's love for you is bigger than the trees; it's taller than the mountains and wider than the seas. God loves you more than the stars or the sun, and to show you his love, he sent his precious Son! God loves us so much, he sent his Son Jesus so he could be with us all the time. God wanted to be near us, to help us, and hear us. God wanted to be closer than a whisper to the ear, so he sent his Son Jesus to stay with us here. Jesus is with us all the time so we never have to feel alone or afraid.

God made a promise to always be with us. How do we know? The Bible tells us so!

Jeremiah 30:11

A Rhyme to Say

God has given us a special gift—the gift of Jesus and the gift of always being with us. God loves us and wants to be with us all the time, every hour of the day, come rain or shine. Isn't it a wonderful gift to know that the Lord is with us all the time, rain or shine?

You can repeat this action rhyme and think about God's special gift of always being near.

Hickory, dickory, dock—
(make your arms "tick" like clock hands)

God is with me around the clock.
(make arm circles)

Rain or shine, all the time—
(make rain motions with your fingers, then put your hands over your head)

Hickory, dickory, dock!
(make your arms "tick" like clock hands again)

Tell about a time that God was with you. Thank God for being with you around the clock!

A Prayer to Pray

Make a shadow on the wall. Can you make the shadow move up and down and dance around? Shadows seem to follow us wherever we go, but shadows stay with us only in the light. Jesus stays with us all the time, day or night, dark or light. Let's praise Jesus for being with us all the time by saying, "Thank you, Lord," after each line.

Jesus is with us; Jesus is here.
Thank you, Lord.
Jesus will help us; Jesus is near.
Thank you, Lord.
Jesus is mighty; Jesus is love.
Thank you, Lord.
We praise you, Jesus, in heaven above!
Thank you, Lord.

Here's a prayer for us to pray to thank God for being with us every day!

Dear God, I'm glad you're with me night and day
And that Jesus stays beside me in sleep or play.
I know you're with me because you love me so,
Please stay beside me wherever I may go. Amen.

About whom did Jesus tell the temple teachers? Find three scrolls.

64

Love to Learn

Jesus said, "Learn from me." Matthew 11:29

A Story to Read

Can you name these letters? J-E-S-U-S. Someone has taught you these letters and you learned them. The letters J-E-S-U-S spell the name of the very best teacher. Do you know what they spell? They spell Jesus' name!

When Jesus was a young boy, he went to the temple to learn about God and to teach others about him. Jesus taught the teachers at the temple about God. The teachers were amazed as they "oohed" and they "ahhed." Imagine a young boy teaching so much about God! But Jesus knew that people needed to learn about God from him. How do we know? The Bible tells us so!

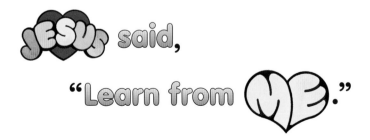

JESUS said,

"Learn from ME."

Matthew 11:29

A Song to Sing

I know a gift that's fun to receive in any kind of weather; it's a gift that never wears out and always lasts forever. What gift am I talking about? Why, the gift of learning that Jesus gives us! Jesus helps us learn important lessons that we can use to help us know God and get along with our family and friends.

Let's sing about Jesus—the best teacher we have!

JESUS TEACHES
(tune: *The Alphabet Song*)

A-B-C-D-E-F-G—
Jesus teaches you and me.

He's our teacher and our friend—
I want his class to never end!

A-B-C-D-E-F-G—
Jesus teaches you and me.

How is Night-Light learning about God? Find the mouse.

A Prayer to Pray

Let's praise and thank Jesus for teaching us. You can say, "We thank you, Jesus," after each line.

For teaching us that God is love,
We thank you, Jesus.
For helping us serve our Father above,
We thank you, Jesus.
For teaching us how to love one another,
We thank you, Jesus.
For helping us learn to forgive each other,
We thank you, Jesus.
For being the best teacher we will ever know,
We thank you, Jesus.
We praise you, Jesus, and love you so!
We thank you, Jesus.

Here's a prayer that we can pray to ask Jesus to teach us every day.

Dear Lord, we want to learn about you
So we will be wise in all that we do.
Please help us and teach us every day
In all that we do and each word we say. Amen.

What were Peter and Andrew doing when they chose to follow Jesus? Find the fishing boat and crab.

Follow-Me Fishermen

Jesus said, "Follow me." Matthew 4:19

A Story to Read

March around the room to this rhyme: hop in the air, then clap one time. Stop your marching, turn around in place, now put a grin across your face. Clap three times, pat your head, hop two hops, then crawl in bed! You're good at following directions. Jesus wants us to follow him and listen to his directions, too.

One day, Jesus met two brothers whose names were Peter and Andrew. Jesus invited these two fishermen to follow him. Peter and Andrew followed Jesus because they knew that Jesus would teach them about God. Jesus wants us to follow him, too. How do we know? The Bible tells us so!

Jesus said, "Follow ME."

Matthew 4:19

A Song to Sing

Weren't Peter and Andrew smart to follow Jesus? The two wise fishermen knew what to do; they followed Jesus—wouldn't you, too? Choosing to follow Jesus is a smart thing to do.

We can sing a song you know. It's all about following the Leader we love and being led by him to our Father above!

FISHERS OF MEN
(traditional song)

**I will make you fishers of men,
Fishers of men, fishers of men!
I will make you fishers of men,
if you follow me!
If you follow me;
if you follow me—
I will make you fishers of men,
if you follow me!**

Find the matching pairs of fish.

A Prayer to Pray

Cut out a paper fish and tape it to your shirt. Now hop around and touch your toes. What did your fish do as you moved? It followed you! Let's praise Jesus for helping us be good followers, too. After each line, say, "I can follow, too!"

Jesus brings love to me and you.
I can follow, too.
Jesus was kind and helpful, too.
I can follow, too.
Jesus told others about God above,
I can follow, too.
And of our Father's forgiving love.
I can follow, too.
Jesus praised God's perfect name,
I can follow, too.
And teaches us to do the same!
I can follow, too.

Here's a prayer for me and you so we can tell Jesus we're his followers, too!

Dear Lord, you're our Leader perfect and true,
And we want to be your followers, too.
Please help us to follow in every way,
And to be like you in all we do and say. Amen.

What did Jesus do when the disciples were afraid? Count the lightning bolts. Find the red belt.

Have No Fear!

Jesus said, "Don't be afraid." Matthew 10:31

A Story to Read

What are you afraid of? Could it be spiders that cause you to shake or is it the dark that makes you quake? Jesus' friends were afraid one dark, stormy night. They were sailing along so peacefully when a storm came upon them suddenly. They thought the boat would sink down, down, down, and that they just might drown, drown, drown. But, who was with them in the boat and had the power to keep them afloat? Jesus was there! Jesus stopped the storm and calmed the waves and his disciples were no longer afraid.

Jesus wants us to trust him and not to be afraid. How do we know? The Bible tells us so!

Jesus said, "Don't bee afraid."

Matthew 10:31

A Rhyme to Say

When we trust Jesus to help us and ask him to take away our fears, he does! Let's enjoy this fun rhyme about not being afraid.

Thunder—pfoo!
(wrinkle your nose)
Lightning, too!
(wrinkle your nose)
I am not afraid of you!
(shake your head)
Spiders—pfoo!
(wrinkle your nose)
Darkness, too!
(wrinkle your nose)
I am not afraid of you!
(shake your head)
I won't shiver and I won't shake
(shake your head)
'Cuz Jesus said, "Don't be afraid."
(waggle your finger)

How many spots are on the butterfly? Find the ladybug.

A Prayer to Pray

We can praise and thank Jesus for taking away our fears so we won't be afraid and so we can feel good about all God has made. Say, "I thank you, Lord" after each phrase.

For being with us night and day,
I thank you, Lord.
For taking every fear away,
I thank you, Lord.
For your strength and perfect power,
I thank you, Lord.
For helping us through every hour,
I thank you, Lord.
For being bigger than any fear,
I thank you, Lord.
I love you, Lord, and hold you dear!

Now here's a prayer for us to pray to thank Jesus for taking our fears away.

Dear God, sometimes we feel afraid
And need a loving touch.
We're thankful you are with us
And that you love us so very much! Amen.

*What is in the basket? Find the cucumber pie,
a salad, a hotdog, ketchup, and a fork.*

Heart Full of Help

Jesus said, "Help other people freely." Matthew 10:8

A Story to Read

I gobbled a hotdog and salad, too, with lots of seeds and dressing and goo. I munched a mound of cucumber pie that was topped with whipped cream a mile high! I wish I had shared my dinner.

Jesus shared a meal with many hungry people. There were 5,000 tummies rumbling and growling. But there was only one small boy with one basket of food. How could five small fish and two loaves of bread feed such a hungry brood? Jesus blessed the boy's offering of help and the small bit of food became a feast of love! Jesus wants us to help others, too! How do we know? The Bible tells us so!

JESUS said, "Help other freely."

Matthew 10:8

A Song to Sing

Here's a song to sing about helping one another!

DID YOU EVER HELP ANOTHER?
(tune: *Did You Ever See a Lassie?*)

Did you ever help another—
Your sister or brother?
Did you ever help another
with your loving heart?
Through kindness and caring
And sweet words and sharing—
Did you ever help another
with your loving heart?

Did you ever help another—
Your daddy or mother?
Did you ever help another
with your loving heart?
By washing the dishes
Or your hugs and kisses—
Did you ever help another
with your loving heart?

*How is Night-Light
helping his friend?*

A Prayer to Pray

A cookie is yummy when there's only one. But sharing a cookie is even more fun! Break a cookie in half and share it as you read this rhyme. Praise Jesus for helping you care for others.

A piece for you and a piece for me—
(share the cookie pieces)
Helps share the fun deliciously!
(give high fives)
Don't keep the fun inside of you—
(waggle your finger)
Care and share with others, too!
(give high fives)
We can help others and do our parts—
(point to someone else)
By helping and healing with love in our hearts!
(point to yourself)

Here's a prayer for us to pray to ask Jesus to help us help others every day.

Dear God, you help us all of our days
And show us your love in millions of ways.
Please help us find ways to help others, too,
And show them our loving kindness, too. Amen.

Who stopped to help the man who was hurt
in Jesus' story? Now find the bandage,
the skunk, a rose, and clover.

Kindness Counts!

Jesus said, "Show mercy." Luke 6:36

A Story to Read

Once I helped a little skunk that no one wanted to; I pulled a splinter off his nose and then he sneezed, "ahh-choo!" I helped because Jesus wants us to show mercy and kindness to others—even people no one else will help!

Jesus told a story about a man who lay hurt in the road. He needed help in a bad way, but only one man stopped to help that day. A man on a donkey came riding by, clip-clip-clop. And because that man had love in his heart, he decided to stop. The Good Samaritan on the donkey helped the hurt man and showed him kindness and mercy. Jesus wants us to show we care and help when someone needs us there. How do we know? The Bible tells us so!

Jesus said,

"Show mercy."

Luke 6:36

A Game to Play

Here's a fun game to remind you how good it is to help others. Hop on your pillow donkey and clippity-clippy-clop; and always remember that kindness never stops!

Trot-trot, clip-clop—
(ride your pillow)
Love and kindness never stop!
(pat your heart)
Jesus teaches us the way
(point upward)
To offer kindness every day!
(give the air a victory punch)

If someone needs your help today,
Trot right up, then smile and say,
"Jesus sent me to help you,
And that is what I'm going to do!"

Trot-trot, clip-clop—
(ride your pillow)
Love and kindness never stop!
(pat your heart)

What kind thing can you do
for someone who needs help?

A Prayer to Pray

Let's praise and thank Jesus for helping us show mercy and kindness to others. After each line, you can say, "We thank you, Lord."

For giving us kind words to say,
God is good.
For showing us your loving ways,
God is good.
For guiding us to be wise and strong,
God is good.
In helping others who come along,
God is good.
For giving us tender hearts that care,
God is good.
So we can help others who need us there,
God is good.
We praise your loving name!

Here's a prayer for us to say to be kind and helpful every day.

Dear God, I'm glad you teach us the way
To be kind and merciful every day.
Help us help others who need us there,
And show there's someone who cares. Amen.

What did the shepherd do when one of his
sheep was lost? Can you help him find his lost sheep?
Find the sheep with the red bow.

Lost and Found

Jesus said, "I will be with you always." Matthew 28:20

A Story to Read

How many sheep can you count with me? 1 sheep, 2 sheep, look, there's 3! 4, 5, 6 sheep—7, 8, 9 . . . Each sheep is precious and fluffy-fine! Jesus told a story about a shepherd with 100 sheep. The shepherd loved all his sheep, so when one sheep became lost, the shepherd searched. He looked up and down and all around 'til his fluffy sheep was finally found. The shepherd loved that lamb and wanted it close to him.

That's just how Jesus loves us. And because Jesus loves us so much, he's with us all the time! How do we know? The Bible tells us so!

Jesus said, " 👁 will 🐝 with U always."

Matthew 28:20

A Rhyme to Say

Just as glue sticks things together, we're stuck like glue to Jesus and he's stuck to us with love! Here's a fun rhyme for you to say to remind you that Jesus is with you each day!

Stuck like glue, stuck like glue—
Jesus' love is stuck to you!
It can't come loose or melt away
'Cuz Jesus' love is here to stay!

Stuck like glue, stuck like glue—
We want to be stuck to Jesus, too!
We can love him every day
And say, "I love you!" when we pray!

Jesus is with me on my bike and when I hike. Where does Jesus go with you?

A Prayer to Pray

Give someone you love a kiss if he's near, and tell that someone you're glad he's here. Isn't it nice to be with the people you love? Let's praise and thank Jesus for being with us all the time.

For being with us when we're up or down;
  (stretch up, then squat down)
For holding us when we're lost, then found;
  (hide your eyes, then open them wide)
For staying close to us day or night;
  (pretend to sleep)
For loving us with all your might;
  (hug yourself)
For wanting us near as a heartbeat to you;
  (pat your heart)
We praise you, dear Jesus, and thank you, too!
  (blow a kiss upward)

Here's a prayer for you to pray to thank Jesus for staying beside you each day.

Dear Lord, I am so glad you're here
And that you always want me near.
You stay beside me, this I know,
And it's because you love me so. Amen.

What did Jesus say about the children?
Find the freckles, the red hair, the green shirt.

Jesus Loves Kids!

Jesus said, "Come to me." Matthew 19:14

A Story to Read

How old are you? What color is your hair? Do you have freckles on your nose or are they barely there? Is your name Martha or Emily or Jim? It doesn't matter who you are—Jesus wants you to come to him! Jesus loves everyone, but he especially loves children just like you!

Once when Jesus was teaching a crowd of people, children came to him. Some people worried that Jesus wouldn't want kids around. Do you know what Jesus said? Jesus said, "Come to me! Let the little children come!" Jesus wants kids all around because he loves them—every one! I'm so glad that Jesus wants me close to him each day! How do we know? The Bible tells us so!

Jesus said, "Come 2 me."

Matthew 19:14

A Song to Sing

Jesus wants us to know and love him as much as he loves us. That's why Jesus wants us to come to him. Let's sing a new song to tell Jesus we want to be near.

COME TO ME

(tune: *Deck the Halls*)

Jesus says, "Now come to me!"
Falalalala—lala—la—la!
That's just where I want to be—
Falalalala—lala—la—la!

Jesus' love will set us free—
Falala—falala—la—la—la!
Jesus loves us all you see!
Falalalala—lala—la—la!

Jesus wants all children to be close to him.
How many children are in this picture?

A Prayer to Pray

When we learn about Jesus and read the Bible and pray, we move closer to Jesus in every way. Let's praise and thank Jesus for wanting us near him. Each time you move, say, "Jesus says, 'Come to me!'"

Take two steps forward as quick as can be—
Jesus says, "Come to me!"
Take two baby steps forward for you and me—
Jesus says, "Come to me!"
Take a giant hop forward, then you'll see—
Jesus says, "Come to me!"
Take three steps forward on your knee—
Jesus says, "Come to me!"
Now praise Jesus with a heart that's free!
Jesus says, "Come to me!"
Yippee!

Let's say a prayer to thank Jesus for loving us and wanting us to be so near.

Dear God, I'm so glad
That you love kids and tots;
And that you want us near
Because you love us lots. Amen.

Who did Zacchaeus want to see when he climbed up in that very tall tree? Find the coin bag and count the coins.

Forgiven for Love

Jesus said, "Forgive other people." Luke 6:37

A Story to Read

Have you ever forgiven someone? It feels nice to forgive
others and it makes them feel good, too.

Do you remember Zacchaeus, who wasn't very tall? He
was a greedy tax collector who was mean to one and all.
He treated people unkindly each day that he was living—
and even though Zacchaeus was awful, Jesus was forgiving!
Jesus forgave Zacchaeus and guess what happened then?
Zacchaeus liked the people and was nice to all of them!
Jesus wants us to forgive people when they say or do
wrong things. How do we know? The Bible tells us so!

Jesus said,

"4 give other ."

Luke 6:37

A Song to Sing

When we offer someone our forgiveness, we also give them the gifts of love and kindness. We all make mistakes, it's true—so you can forgive me and I'll forgive you! And the best part? Jesus will forgive us, too!

Let's sing a song about being kind and forgiving to one another.

THE KINDNESS SONG

(tune: *Ten Little Indians*)

Be kind and loving to one another,
Be forgiving of each other—

Show your love in all you do
'Cuz that's how God loves you!

Oh-oh! What will Night-Light need to ask Teddy to do? How can you be kind like Night-Light and Teddy?

A Prayer to Pray

Give a "thumbs down" if the phrase is about being mean, and a "thumbs up" if the phrase is about forgiving others.

If someone calls me a mean, nasty name,
(thumbs down)
I will forgive them and not do the same!
(thumbs up)
If somebody bops me or pushes me around,
(thumbs down)
I will forgive them and not push them down!
(thumbs up)
I'll praise Jesus, for I know that it's true,
(thumbs up)
"If you forgive others who aren't nice to you—
(thumbs down)
Our loving Lord will forgive you, too!"
(thumbs up)

Here's a prayer for us to pray to be more forgiving every day.

Dear God, we know you made the earth
And all the stars above.
You made the world then added us
So you'd have someone to love! Amen.

How did the people welcome Jesus when he came to town? Find these colored robes: yellow, blue, orange.

Welcome, Jesus!

Jesus said, "Be ready!" Luke 12:40

A Story to Read

Do you have a "Welcome" mat outside your door?
Welcome mats greet people when they come to see you.
It's nice to give others a warm welcome, isn't it?

Long ago, Jesus was going to visit the town of
Jerusalem. The people got all ready for Jesus to come and
planned a very warm welcome. They placed their robes on
the ground and Jesus rode over them on his way to town.
The people waved palm branches in the air to show Jesus
they were glad that he was there. When we get ready for
Jesus, we put love in our hearts, read God's Word, and
obey all God says. Jesus wants us to be ready for him
today! How do we know? The Bible tells us so!

Jesus said, " ready!"

Luke 12:40

A Rhyme to Say

Let's use the words "well" and "come" to welcome Jesus into our hearts and tell him we love him.

Well come, Jesus,
(motion as if saying, "come here")
into my heart—
(pat your heart)
I welcome you right from the start!
(hop in the air)
I want you beside me
(pat your side)
Each day and each night.
(pretend to sleep)
I want to obey you
(point upward)
And always do right.
(nod your head)
Well come, Jesus,
(motion as if saying, "come here")
into my heart—
(pat your heart)
I welcome you right from the start!
(hop in the air)

Can you name the letters on the welcome mat?

A Prayer to Pray

Cut out a big paper leaf. Can you wave your leaf back and forth? This is what the people did to welcome Jesus into their city. We welcome Jesus with the love and trust our hearts can raise, and we welcome Jesus with our thanks and praise! Wave your paper leaf when you hear the word "hosanna."

Hosanna, hosanna—get ready for Jesus!
For he is the one who loves and frees us!

Hosanna, hosanna—our hearts are raised,
For Jesus is Lord and greatly to be praised!

Hosanna, hosanna—let's welcome our Jesus,
For he is the one who loves and frees us!

Here's a prayer for us to pray to get ready for Jesus right away.

Dear Lord, make our hearts ready so you know
How welcome you are and we love you so!
We want you in our lives in every way
To love us and guide us every day! Amen.

How did Jesus' friends feel when they found out he was alive?
How many happy faces can you count?

Jesus Is Alive!

Jesus said, "I will be with you always." Matthew 28:20

A Story to Read

Jesus' friends must have sung a happy song on the morning they found out that Jesus was alive! Jesus had died to forgive our sins. Oh, how sad Jesus' friends had been. Three days after Jesus died—1, 2, 3—Jesus' friends went to his tomb and bent to peek inside. What do you think they saw? Nothing! That's because Jesus was raised from death to be with God. And Jesus promises to be with us forever.

Jesus promised that he would always be right beside both you and me! How do we know? The Bible tells us so.

A Song to Sing

Let's sing a special song to celebrate the wonderful news that Jesus is alive! You can even make up more actions and verses on your own!

Jesus is alive today!
Clap your hands and shout "Hooray!"
Jesus is alive today, and forevermore!

Jesus is alive today!
Twirl around and shout "Hooray!"
Jesus is alive today, and forevermore!

Jesus is alive today!
Pat your toes and shout "Hooray!"
Jesus is alive today, and forevermore!

Night-Light is praising Jesus with a song. Which instruments can you name?

A Prayer to Pray

I'm sure Jesus' friends couldn't keep from singing praises to our Lord. We can praise Jesus, too! After each line, clap and say, "I'll clap my hands and praise you, Lord!"

Because I love and treasure you,
I'll clap my hands and praise you, Lord!
For all the wondrous things you do,
I'll clap my hands and praise you, Lord!
Because you gave your life for me,
I'll clap my hands and praise you, Lord!
Because you promise to stay with me,
I'll clap my hands and praise you, Lord!
For showing me the way to our Father above,
I'll clap my hands and praise you, Lord!
Because you're alive and you give me your love,
I'll clap my hands and praise you, Lord!

Now here's a prayer for you to pray to praise Jesus for being with us today.

Dear Lord, when you died for us we felt sadness,
But now there's only joy and gladness!
For you are Lord and we can say,
"We're so glad you're alive today!" Amen.

What happened when Peter prayed while he was in jail?

Pray Each Day

Jesus said, "Ask and you will receive." John 16:24

A Story to Read

Once I was lost in the grocery store. I couldn't find Mommy anywhere! I thought I'd give God a prayer, but would he hear me even there? He did! Mommy found me and I found that God helps me wherever I am if I ask him.

Long ago, Peter found out that God hears and helps anywhere, too! Peter was in jail for telling others about Jesus. But Peter prayed and so did his friends. They asked God to help Peter through their prayers, but Peter was in jail; would God help him even there? He did! God sent angels to free Peter so he could keep telling people about Jesus.

Jesus wants us to ask God for his help. And Jesus knows that God will help when we ask him. How do we know? The Bible tells us so!

JESUS said,

"Ask and U will receive."

John 16:24

A Song to Sing

God will always answer us and help us when we ask him! Jesus promised that when we ask God for his help through prayer, we will receive his loving help—any time and anywhere! Just like Peter, we can trust God to help us when we ask him.

Let's sing God a happy song to thank him for taking the time to hear and answer us.

GOD WILL ANSWER

(tune: *Jesus Loves Me*)

**God will hear and answer us
Because he loves and cares for us—
God will answer in his way
When we bow our hearts to pray.
Yes, God will answer—
Yes, God will answer—
Yes, God will answer—
Because he loves us so.**

What does Night-Light remember to do when he needs some help?

A Prayer to Pray

God likes it when we talk to him in prayer and he promises to help us anytime or anywhere! Let's praise and thank God for his help and love.

One little prayer I say to God above.
(hold up one finger)
Two hands clap when he answers me with love.
(clap your hands)
Three words I'll say to God when I pray—
Please help me!
Four words of thanks when he answers right away—
Thank you very much.
Five important words we can always believe,
(hold up 5 fingers)
Were said by Jesus, "Ask and you will receive."

Now here's a prayer for us to pray to remember to ask for God's help each day.

Dear Lord, when we need help
All we have to do is pray,
And you will hear and answer us
Anytime night or day! Amen.

God bless you and good night!

Scripture Index